Sekiya Miyoshi

Daniel and the Lion

THE
PILGRIM
PRESS

Cleveland

A long time ago, Daniel lived in a desert country. Each night, when Daniel slept, he had many strange dreams.

And somehow all his dreams always seemed to come true.

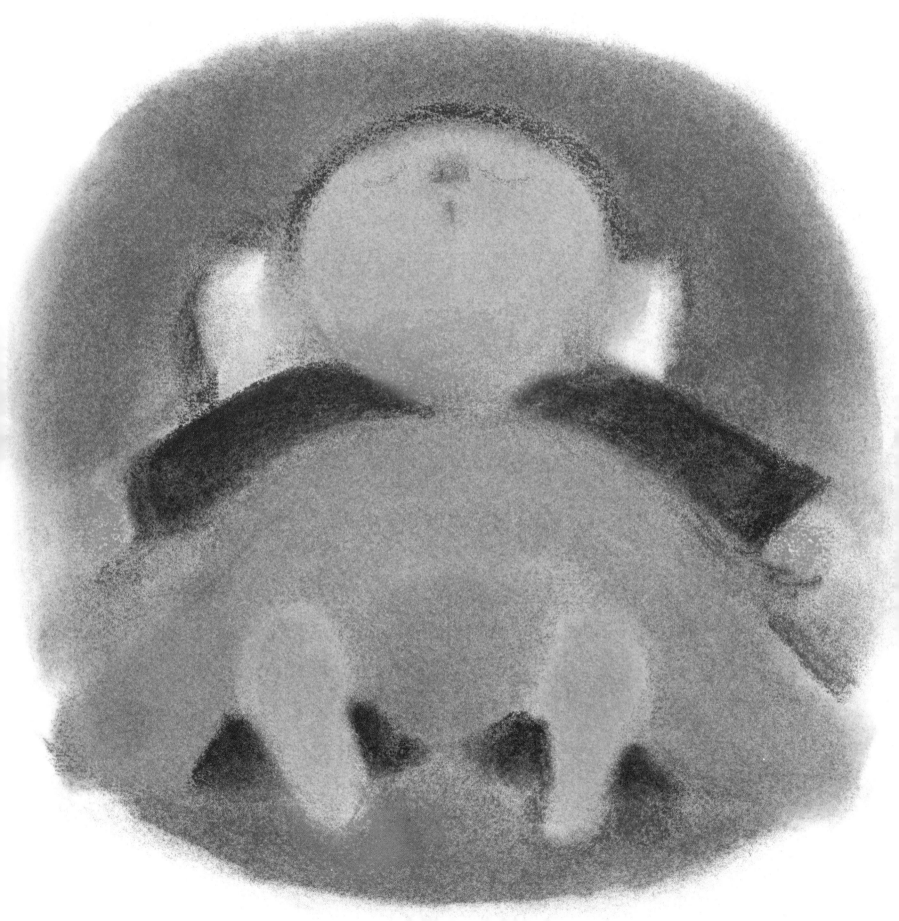

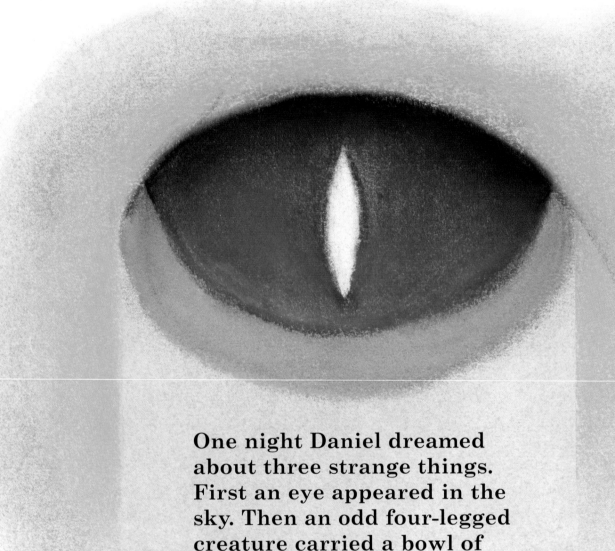

One night Daniel dreamed
about three strange things.
First an eye appeared in the
sky. Then an odd four-legged
creature carried a bowl of
water. Finally a flute with
wings fluttered about.

That next morning, Daniel told his dream to his friends, the cat, the bird, and the camel. "Cat," he said, "last night I dreamed of an eye in the sky. Now I see that it was your eye. Bird, last night I dreamed of a flute with wings. Now I see that it was you, flying through the air. Camel, you are like a ship in the desert as you can journey a long way with water in your hump. I dreamed of you, too." His friends were pleased.

Just then Daniel pointed. "Look," he said. "Someone is coming."

The king's messenger was speeding on horseback across the sand.
"The king needs your help."

Daniel and Cat walked across the sand to the king's palace. A huge, golden statue of the king stood at the entrance. People were kneeling round it and worshiping it because the king banned worship or prayer to God.

Like Daniel, the king sometimes had strange dreams when he slept. He wanted to know what they meant.
Daniel told the king so much about his dreams, and Daniel told it so well, that the king was pleased. He gave Daniel many presents.
This made some people jealous.

Each morning and evening, Daniel thanked God with all his heart.

Those jealous of Daniel noticed that Daniel prayed to God and not to the golden statue as the king had ordered all to do.

They told the king, who became very angry. "Cast Daniel into the lions' den," he commanded.

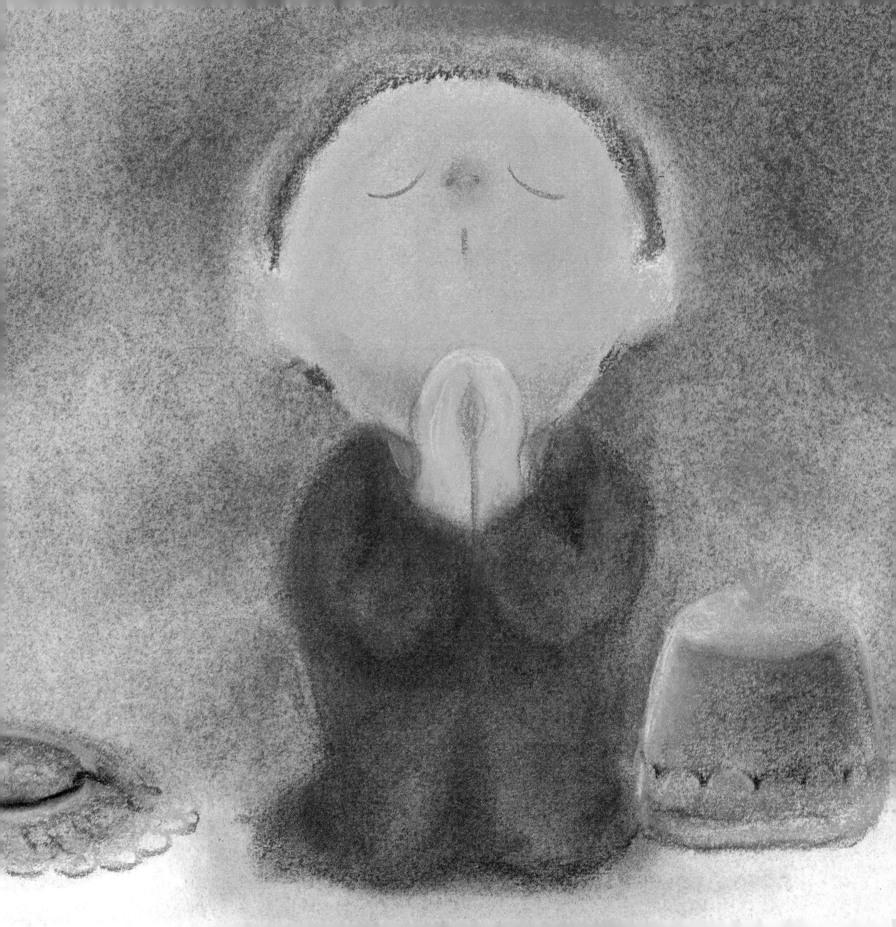

So Daniel was tossed in among the lions.

A big lion—the oldest of all those in the den—rushed to Daniel. "Are you scared?" the lion snarled. "I am very hungry!" He showed his teeth, and his claws were ready to tear Daniel into pieces.
"Don't eat me tonight, please," Daniel said, looking into the lion's eyes. "You may eat me tomorrow morning. Tonight I want to have dreams one last time."
Daniel then prayed to God to save him. The lion snarled again, but left Daniel alone.

Daniel told the lions
all about his dreams.
The little lion cubs
asked, "Why can't
we have dreams?"

"If you pray to God, perhaps God will also send you dreams," Daniel replied.

"Who is God?" asked the cubs. Daniel told them all about God, who is the maker of all things in the world.

That night, Daniel slept among the lions.
They made a big circle around him, and he
curled up with the cubs in the center.

That night, they all had dreams. Each dream was a happy one.

Meanwhile, the king in his palace was unhappy to think that the lions would eat Daniel.

But in the morning, look! Daniel came out of the lion's den, safe and sound. The king was amazed. The jealous people were amazed! Even the lions said to themselves, "Oh my, we forgot to eat Daniel."

The king was so happy to see Daniel alive. He knew that Daniel's God must be the true one. The king saw how happy the animals were and thought, "Daniel's God can make my people happy as well." As the king and Daniel prayed together, Cat and a lion cub slept near them. A camel slept under a palm tree. All their dreams were happy ones.

First published in North America 2001
by The Pilgrim Press
700 Prospect Aveue
Cleveland, Ohio 44115-1100 U.S.A.
pilgrimpress.com
Illustration and Original Text
Copyright © 1982 by Hisae Miyoshi
Original Japanese Edition "Danieru"
published in 1982 by
Shiko-Sha Co. Ltd., Tokyo, Japan
English text © 2001 The Pilgrim Press
Printed in China
06 05 04 03 02 01   1 2 3 4 5
ISBN 0-8298-1452-3